21-Day Devotional & Confession Guide

Recognizing When God Speaks:

A Journey into How the Lord Uses Us to Guide, Affirm, and Reveal His Will

Jacquatta J Jones, Psy.D.

RECOGNIZING WHEN GOD SPEAKS

21-DAY DEVOTIONAL & CONFESSION GUIDE

ISBN: 9798234046451

Printed in the United States of America

Published by: Power of Meditation/God

Contents

Introduction... 9

Day 1-When God Speaks in the Night...............21

Day 2-The Language of Dreams and
       Symbols..25

Day 3-Fear Breaks When Faith Speaks............31

Day 4-Obedience Unlocks Purpose 35

Day 5-Tested, Then Trusted 39

Day 6-From Fearful to Faithful 43

Day 7-Intercession Begins with
       Compassion...................................47

Day 8-When God Uses the Whole-Body..........51

Day 9-Discernment of Atmosphere 57

Day 10-Praying Past the Pain 61

Day 11-Confirmation and Clarity....................65

Day 12-Spiritual Sensitivity 69

Day 13-Discerning the Atmosphere 73

Day 14-The Power of Stillness........................77

Day 15-Meditating on the Word....................... 81

Day 16-Meditation as a Lifestyle 85

Day 17-From Meditation to Manifestation...... 89

Day 18-The Fragrance of Worship..................93

Day 19-Prayer That Listens............................97

Day 20-Intercession That Changes
        Atmospheres.. 101

Day 21-Keep Listening:
        A Life Led by His Voice........................ 105

Before You Begin:

Preparing to Hear God's Voice

Before you begin your 21-day journey, take a deep breath and quiet all other distractions.

God is still speaking-not only to prophets, but to all His children who are willing to listen. His voice comes through His Word, through dreams, through inner impressions, and sometimes through silence that carries weight.

To recognize when God speaks, you must first posture your heart.

The Word reminds us in Psalm 105:4, "Seek the Lord and His strength; seek His face evermore." Seeking His face means prioritizing relationships over results. It means coming to Him, not for what He can give, but for who He is.

The Hebrew word and meaning of "seek" here is baqas: to seek to find; to require, exact; to desire, demand; to ask, request.

As you read each day, expect revelation. Expect the Holy Spirit to personalize truth for your life.

Keep a journal nearby-what you capture in writing often becomes the evidence of God's faithfulness later.

Prayer:

Father God, in the Name of Jesus, I remove all other distractions, fears assumptions and doubt. Open my spiritual ears to discern Your whispers and align my heart with Your will. In Jesus's name, Amen

Declaration:

I am ready to hear. My heart is open, my mind is clear, and my spirit is attentive to Your voice, Lord.

Introduction:

Acknowledging the One True God

Before we go any further, I pause to acknowledge **God—the Creator of the universe**, the One who spoke light into existence and stretched out the heavens with His breath. He is the **I AM**, the self-existent One, the One who was, who is, and who is to come.[1]

I honor **His name**, the name above every name—**YHWH**, the covenant-keeping God who reveals Himself to His people. I acknowledge **Jesus Christ**, the Son of God, the Word made flesh, the One through whom all things were created and by whom all things are sustained. And I honor the **Holy Spirit**, the Spirit of Truth who dwells within us, leads us, speaks to us, and makes the voice of God unmistakably clear.

These three are not separate but triune.
They are **One**—Father, Son, and Holy Spirit—perfect in unity, perfect in purpose, perfect in power.

Who Is God?

God is the eternal, sovereign, self-existent Creator.
He has no beginning and no end. He is Spirit, He is Holy, and He is Love. He is the source of all wisdom, all life, all truth, and every breath you breathe.

He is the Father who created you.
He is the Son who redeemed you.
He is the Holy Spirit who dwells within you.

God reveals Himself through His names:

- **Elohim** – Creator and Powerful One
- **YHWH / Yahweh** – The Eternal "I AM"
- **Adonai** – Lord and Master
- **El Shaddai** – The All-Sufficient God
- **Jehovah-Shalom** – The God of Peace
- **Jehovah-Rohi** – The Lord My Shepherd
- **Jehovah-Rapha** – The Lord Who Heals
- **Jehovah-Jireh** – The Lord Who Provides

And He revealed Himself most clearly in the person of **Jesus Christ**, "who is the exact image of the invisible God the firstborn of every creature" (Colossians 1:15).

When we ask, *"Who is God?"* we are not asking
an intellectual question—we are asking a relational
one.
God is the One who formed you, called you,
guides you, speaks to you, and desires to walk with
you.

He is the One who invites you into fellowship…
The One who reveals mysteries…
The One who heals broken places…
The One who whispers direction in the quiet
moments of your day.

God is not distant. He is present.
God is not silent. He is speaking.
**God is not hidden. He is revealing Himself to
those who listen.**

This devotional journey begins with honoring
Him—Father, Son, and Holy Spirit—the God who
still speaks.

Scripture Focus:

Psalm 46:10 (NLT)

"Be still, and know that I am God! I will be honored by every nation. I will be honored throughout the world."

It reminds us that in the middle of chaos, uncertainty, or noise, God invites us to stop striving and trust Him. He is faithful, and He will be exalted above every situation. It is an invitation to experience peace by remembering who He is.

Psalm 46:10 Summary:

God is calling His people to be still-to stop striving, worrying, and trying to control things-and to recognize that He alone is God. He is sovereign over every nation, every situation, and every circumstance. The verse is a reminder to trust His power, rest in His presence, and allow Him to be exalted in the earth and in our lives.

Devotional Reflection:

There are moments when God's voice is not found in the thunder or the whirlwind but in the stillness. He speaks in whispers that reach the core of our hearts when the noise of the world fades away. Many times, we miss His voice not because He isn't speaking, but because we haven't paused long enough to listen.

When you quiet your thoughts, your fears, and your need to have all the answers, the Lord will begin to reveal His will with clarity. This is where relationships deepen in the still place of trust.

Ask yourself: "What might God be whispering to me in this season?"

Prayer:

Heavenly Father, teach me to be still before You. Silence every voice that competes with Yours. Help me to recognize when You are speaking and to respond with faith and obedience. In every quiet moment, let my spirit rest in Your presence. In Jesus's name, amen.

Reflection:

- What distractions do I need to silence so I can better hear God's voice?
- How does God usually get my attention?
- What step of obedience is He prompting me to take today?

Key Insight from the Book:

"God's voice brings peace, not confusion. When He speaks, His message aligns with His Word, His character, and His love for you."

Recognizing When God Speaks
Dr. Jacquatta J. Jones

Journal:

How to Use This Devotional:

Recognizing When God Speaks: 21-Day Devotional & Confession Guide

This devotional was created to help you **develop spiritual sensitivity, deepen your relationship with God, and grow in confidence in recognizing His voice**. Each day is designed to guide you through Scripture, reflection, prayer, and confession so that you can intentionally meditate on God's presence.

1. Set Aside Dedicated Time

Choose a consistent time each day to engage with the devotional. Many people find early morning or quiet evening moments most effective because distractions are minimal, and the heart is more receptive.

2. Begin with Prayer

Before reading, invite the Holy Spirit to open your understanding. Ask God to help you hear His voice clearly and to reveal what He desires to show you through His Word.

3. Read the Scripture Slowly

Each day begins with a key Scripture. Read it carefully and allow the words to settle in your spirit. Sometimes reading the verse more than once helps deepen your understanding.

4. Reflect on the Teaching

The teaching reflection will help you understand the spiritual principle connected to the Scripture. Take time to consider how the message applies to your life and current season.

5. Focus on the Key Insight

The Key Insight highlights the central truth of the day. Let this thought guide your meditation throughout the day.

6. Speak the Confession Aloud

Confessions are powerful because they align your words with God's truth. Speak the daily confession slowly and intentionally. Allow the declaration to renew your mind and strengthen your faith.

7. Pray the Prayer

Use the prayer as a moment to communicate with God personally. Feel free to expand it with your own words as the Holy Spirit leads.

8. Journal What God Reveals

The journal prompt is an opportunity to record thoughts, impressions, dreams, or confirmations you receive. Writing helps capture revelation and allows you to reflect on how God has been speaking throughout the journey.

9. Practice Stillness

After completing the devotional, take a few moments of quiet to listen. Sometimes God speaks most clearly in the silence that follows prayer and meditation.

10. Repeat and Meditate on the Confession Throughout the Day

Carry the confession with you throughout the day. Repeating it strengthens spiritual focus and keeps your heart aligned with what God is revealing.

Final Encouragement

Approach these 21 days with expectation. God still speaks to His people. As you read, meditate, pray, and listen, you will begin to recognize His voice with greater clarity and confidence.

Day 1 – When God Speaks in the Night

Job 33:14–15 (NLT)

"For God speaks again and again, though people do not recognize it. He speaks in dreams, in visions of the night. When deep sleep falls on people as they lie in their beds."

Job 33:14-15 Summary:

God speaks to people in many ways, even when they do not recognize that it is Him. He may speak through quiet warnings, dreams, or visions in night. While a person sleeps, God can give direction, correction, or insight, His voice often working beyond our conscious awareness to guide and protect us

Teaching-Reflection:

Night hours often become the classroom of Heaven. When your body rests, your spirit remains awake to receive revelation. God used dreams to warn Joseph, direct Daniel, and prepare Mary's husband for his assignment. Dreams are not coincidences; they are invitations to partnership.

The Lord still speaks while you sleep, not to entertain but to instruct. Each dream carries symbols that require prayerful discernment, not human guessing. Ask the Holy Spirit, *"What are You revealing to me?"* and wait in faith for understanding.

Key Insight:

Dreams are divine scrolls written on the canvas of your spirit. Interpretation belongs to God, but expectation belongs to you.

Confession to Meditate Upon:

"I receive wisdom and understanding in the night. My dreams are sanctified by the Spirit and filled with divine direction."

Prayer:

Father, thank You for speaking even while I rest. Teach me to recognize Your voice through dreams and to record what You reveal. Guard my mind from confusion and confirm every message through Your Word. In Jesus's name, amen.

Journal:

Describe a dream that stayed with you. What emotion or message lingers? Ask the Holy Spirit for clarity and write what He reveals.

____

____

____

____

____

____

____

____

____

____

____

____

Day 2 – The Language of Dreams and Symbols

Daniel 2:19, 22 (NLT)

"That night the secret was revealed to Daniel in a vision. Then Daniel praised the God of heaven. … He reveals deep and mysterious things and knows what lies hidden in darkness, though he is surrounded by light."

Daniel 2:19, 22 Summary:

God revealed the mystery to Daniel **in a night vision,** showing that divine understanding does not come from human wisdom but from **revelation given by God Himself.** These verses established that **God alone possesses hidden knowledge,** controls darkness, and releases insight at His appointed time.

Daniel 2:22 declares that **God reveals deep and secret things,** meaning nothing is concealed from Him-not mysteries of the future, not matters of the heart, and not the purposes of Heaven. Light dwells with God, and when He chooses, He illuminates what was one hidden so His people can walk in clarity, wisdom, and authority.

Key Truth:

God reveals mysteries to those who seek Him. What is hidden in darkness is not meant to remain hidden forever-God unveils it in His presence.

Teaching-Reflection:

God speaks through imagery because pictures bypass resistance. The language of symbols is Heaven's art form. Joseph saw sheaves bowing, Peter saw a sheet descending from the sky, and John saw golden lampstands—each image held revelation.

When interpreting, never rush. Compare what you see with Scripture and character of Christ. Symbols from God will always produce peace and align with His Word. What confuses or condemns rarely comes from Him.

Key Insight:

Every divine symbol points back to Scripture; every revelation should draw you nearer to the Revealer, not the mystery itself.

Confession to Meditate Upon:

"I walk in divine understanding. The Spirit of truth interprets what God shows me, and my insight glorifies Christ."

Prayer:

Lord, open the eyes of my understanding. Help me discern Your voice through spiritual symbols. Let wisdom rest upon me as it did upon Daniel, so that what You reveal may bring light to others. In Jesus name, amen.

Journal:

Write one symbol that has appeared repeatedly in your dreams or prayers. Search Scripture for its meaning and note how it connects to your current season.

Day 3 – Fear Breaks When Faith Speaks

2 Timothy 1:7 (KJV)

"For God hath not given us the spirit of fear; but of power, and of love, and of a sound mind."

2 Timothy 1:7 Summary:

God makes it unmistakably clear that fear does not originate from Him. Fear is not a personality trait, a weakness, or a calling—it is an intruder. Instead, God has deposited power, love, and a sound (disciplined, self-controlled) mind within His people.

This verse teaches that when fear tries to silence, delay, or intimidate you, it is evidence of a voice that does not belong to God. The presence of God's Spirit produces courage, clarity, and confident action, even in moments of uncertainty.

Key Truth:

If fear is leading, God is not the source. His voice empowers, stabilizes, and strengthens.

Teaching-Reflection:

Fear silences destiny. It disguises itself as caution or humility, but its goal is to mute your voice. Just as Moses hesitated before Pharaoh, many believers delay obedience because they doubt their ability. Yet God never asked for ability; He asked for availability.

Faith is not the absence of trembling; it is the decision to move while trembling. Every time you act on what God says, fear loses territory. Speaking what He speaks restores dominion over your thoughts, words, and confidence.

Key Insight:

Faith activates God's voice in your life; silence strengthens fear's argument. Speak what Heaven decrees until your emotions align.

Confession to Meditate Upon:

"I am bold, confident, and sound-minded. Fear no longer governs me—I speak with the authority of Christ."

Prayer:

Father, thank You for replacing fear with faith. Teach me to see myself as You see me—chosen, equipped, and courageous. Let every word I speak agree with Your promises. In Jesus's name, amen.

Journal:

Identify one area where fear has held you back. Write a declaration of faith to replace it and speak it aloud each morning this week.

____

____

____

____

____

____

____

____

____

Day 4 – Obedience Unlocks Purpose

1 Samuel 15:22 (NIV)

"To obey is better than sacrifice, and to heed is better than the fat of rams."

1 Samuel 15:22 Summary:

God reveals that obedience matters more than outward religious effort. Sacrifice represents what we give, but obedience represents how we listen. This scripture teaches that God values a heart that responds to His voice above rituals, offerings, or good intentions.

Saul's failure shows that partial obedience is still disobedience. God desires alignment, not substitution. When we obey, we demonstrate trust in God's authority and acknowledge that His instruction is wiser than our understanding.

Key Truth:

God honors listening hearts over impressive actions. Obedience proves that we truly hear Him.

Teaching-Reflection:

Obedience is Heaven's love language. God often tests our hearts through simple instructions that seem small but carry eternal weight. When the Holy Spirit nudges you to call someone, sow a seed, or release a word, respond quickly. Delay breeds doubt, and hesitation can rob you of breakthrough.
Your next assignment is hidden inside your last instruction.

Key Insight:

Every act of obedience opens a new level of revelation. The moment you move, Heaven moves with you.

Confession to Meditate Upon:

"I respond swiftly to God's voice. My obedience unlocks doors that sacrifice alone cannot open."

Prayer:

Father, make me quick to obey. Help me discern Your timing and trust Your direction even when it stretches my comfort zone. Let my obedience bring glory to Your name. Amen.

Journal:

What was the last instruction you hesitated to follow? What step can you take today toward obedience?

____

____

____

____

____

____

____

____

____

____

____

____

____

____

Day 5 – Tested, Then Trusted

2 Corinthians 12:9 (NKJV)

"My grace is sufficient for you, for My strength is made perfect in weakness."

2 Corinthians 12:9 Summary:

The Lord reveals that His grace is not given to remove every weakness but to sustain us through it. This verse teaches that human limitation becomes the stage upon which divine power is displayed. Rather than eliminating weakness, God uses it as an opportunity to demonstrate His strength.

When we stop striving to appear strong and instead depend on God, His power rests upon us. Weakness does not disqualify us—it positions us to experience the sufficiency of God's grace. What feels like vulnerability becomes a vessel for His glory.

Key Truth:

God's power is most visible where self-reliance ends. Grace does not just help you endure-it empowers you to overcome.

Teaching-Reflection:

Before every promotion comes a test. God refines character before releasing greater influence. Trials are not punishments—they are preparation. When you pass the test of humility, faith, and perseverance, you become trustworthy with His power.

Key Insight:

Tests reveal the truth of your faith. God promotes based on proven endurance, not potential enthusiasm.

Confession to Meditate Upon:

"I am strengthened by grace and refined through testing. Every trial shapes me for God's glory."

Prayer:

Lord, thank You for trusting me with challenges that mature my spirit. Help me to see trials as divine classrooms, not punishments. May my endurance prove Your faithfulness. Amen.

Journal

What current challenge could God be using to prepare you for a new level of purpose?

Day 6 – From Fearful to Faithful

Philippians 4:13 (NKJV)

"I can do all things through Christ who strengthens me."

Philippians 4:23 Summary:

This verse serves as a spiritual benediction, reminding believers that everything we receive, endure, and overcome is sustained by the grace of the Lord Jesus Christ. Paul closes his letter by emphasizing that grace is not merely a doctrine—it is an active presence that dwells within the believer's spirit.

Grace is what empowers perseverance, produces peace, and keeps the believer anchored regardless of circumstances. This closing blessing affirms that the Christian life is lived from the inside out, sustained by Christ's indwelling grace rather than external conditions.

Key Truth:

Grace is not only God's gift to you—it is God's presence within you, enabling you to live faithfully and finish well.

Teaching-Reflection:

Faith is the antidote to fear. When you declare God's Word in trembling moments, courage rises. Moses learned that his weakness became strength when God's voice filled his mouth. The same Spirit empowers you. Speak the Word until boldness overtakes hesitation.

Key Insight:

Fear retreats where faith speaks. The strength of Christ transforms insecurity into assignment.

Confession to Meditate Upon:

"I am empowered by the Spirit of God. My faith silences fear and propels me into divine purpose."

Prayer:

Father, let Your courage fill every place fear once lived. Teach me to walk in confidence of who I am in You. In Jesus's name, amen.

Journal:

Where is fear limiting your obedience? Write one faith action you will take this week.

____

____

____

____

____

____

____

____

____

____

____

____

____

Day 7 – Intercession Begins with Compassion

Ezekiel 22:30 (NIV)

"I looked for someone among them who would build up the wall and stand before me in the gap on behalf of the land so I would not have to destroy it, but I found no one"

Ezekiel 22:30 Summary:

God searched for someone—an intercessor—who would stand in the gap on behalf of the land. He was looking for a person willing to pray, repent, and contend spiritually so judgment could be averted. But He found no one.

In essence:

The verse reveals the power and responsibility of intercession. One surrendered, obedient person could have made a difference—but the absence of that intercessor led to consequences.

- God looks for people who will build up and stand in the gap
- Silence, passivity, or compromise creates spiritual vulnerability

- Intercession isn't optional; it's a calling that can change outcomes

Teaching-Reflection:

True intercession flows from love, not obligation. The Holy Spirit often burdens your heart for people who may never know you're praying for them. Your compassion becomes the bridge Heaven uses to release mercy.
Every tear shed in prayer is a seed of intercession that will never go unnoticed.

Key Insight:

Intercession is love expressed through prayer. When you carry someone in prayer, you carry the heart of God.

Confession to Meditate Upon:

"I am an intercessor filled with compassion. My prayers release Heaven's mercy into the earth."

Prayer:

Lord, teach me to pray with Your heart. Help me to love even those who have wounded me. Let my intercession birth deliverance for others. In Jesus's name, amen

Journal:

Who has God placed on your heart to pray for this week? How can you show them grace in action?

____

____

____

____

____

____

____

____

____

____

____

____

____

Day 8 – When God Uses the Whole-Body

Proverbs 20:27 (KJV)

"The spirit of man is the candle of the Lord, searching all the inward parts of the belly."

Proverbs 20:27 Summary:

This verse reveals that the human spirit is God's lamp within us.

He uses our spirit as a light to examine, reveal, and search the deepest place of our inner being-our motives, intentions, wounds, desires, and truth.

In Essence:

- Your spirit is not random-it is designed for divine communication.
- God illuminates hidden areas through your spirit.
- Conviction, awareness, inner checks, and spiritual impressions often flow from this inward light.

Key Insight:

(Meditation & Intercession)

The Lord does not always speak from the outside in.

He often speaks from the inside out.

When you meditate, pray in the Spirit, or experience those early-morning awakenings and prophetic body checks, you are witnessing Proverbs 20:27 in motion:-God searching, highlighting, and revealing through your spirit.

Teaching-Reflection:

Sometimes God speaks through sensation—a quickening, a stirring, a physical awareness of His presence. These "body alerts" are invitations to intercede. The Holy Spirit uses your sensitivity as a signal that someone or something needs prayer. Journal these encounters; over time, you'll notice divine patterns.

Key Insight:

Sensitivity to the Spirit is not strange—it's sacred. The more you respond, the more Heaven entrusts.

Confession to Meditate Upon:

"My body is a vessel of divine sensitivity. I respond to the Spirit's alerts with prayer and obedience."

Prayer:

Holy Spirit, thank You for trusting me with spiritual sensitivity. Teach me to discern and respond in wisdom and love. Let every alert lead me to intercession, not fear. In Jesus's name, amen.

Journal

Recall a moment when you felt a physical prompt to pray. What do you believe the Spirit was revealing?

Day 9 – Discernment of Atmosphere

2 Corinthians 2:14–15 (NKJV)

"Now thanks be to God who always leads us in triumph in Christ, and through us diffuses the fragrance of His knowledge in every place."

2 Corinthians 2:14-15 Summary:

In these verses, the Apostle Paul declares that God always causes us to triumph in Christ and uses our lives to spread the fragrance of the knowledge of Him everywhere. Believers are described as a sweet aroma of Christ to God- both among those who are being saved and those who are perishing.

Teaching-Reflection:

Just as natural smoke fills a room, spiritual atmospheres carry fragrance—peace or unrest, purity or pollution. God sharpens your senses to discern what lingers in a space. Don't fear it; address it through prayer and worship. You are the fragrance of Christ wherever you go.

Key Insight:

Discernment isn't suspicion—it's spiritual awareness that empowers transformation.

Confession to Meditate Upon:

"I carry the fragrance of Christ. Darkness cannot remain where the presence of God resides in me."

Prayer:

Father, increase my discernment. Make me aware of spiritual environments without becoming overwhelmed by them. Let my worship shift every atmosphere I enter. In Jesus's name, amen.

Journal:

What spiritual atmosphere have you recently noticed in your home, workplace, or ministry? How might God be asking you to respond?

____

____

____

____

Day 10 – Praying Past the Pain

Matthew 5:44 (NKJV)

"But I say to you, love your enemies, bless those who curse you, do good to those who hate you, and pray for those who spitefully use you."

Matthew 5:44 Summary:

In Matthew 5:44, Jesus commands believers to love their enemies, bless those who curse them, do good to those who hate them, and pray for those who mistreat or persecute them.

- Love is not reserved for those who treat us well.
- Kingdom love responds with grace instead of retaliation.
- Prayer replaces revenge.
- Goodness confronts hatred.

This verse reveals a higher standard of righteousness—one that reflects the heart of the Father. Loving enemies is not emotional agreement; it is a spiritual decision rooted in obedience and maturity.

Teaching-Reflection:

Intercession often requires forgiveness. Sometimes God calls you to pray for those who hurt you—not to justify them, but to heal you. When you release offense, prayer becomes pure. Love is the highest warfare; it conquers what bitterness cannot.

Key Insight:

Forgiveness frees the intercessor first. Love restores power to your prayers.

Confession to Meditate Upon:

"I release every offense. I choose love over retaliation and prayer over resentment."

Prayer:

Lord, soften my heart toward those who have wronged me. Teach me to pray from compassion, not pain. Let my forgiveness become a testimony of Your grace. Amen.

Journal:

Who is God asking you to forgive and pray for today? Write their name and declare blessing over them.

____

____

____

____

____

____

____

____

____

____

____

____

____

____

Day 11 – Confirmation and Clarity

John 14:26 (KJV)

"But the Comforter, which is the Holy Ghost, whom the Father will send in my name, he shall teach you all things, and bring all things to your remembrance whatsoever I have said unto you."

John 14:26 Summary:

- The Holy Spirit is our divine Teacher.
- He provides understanding beyond intellect
- He reminds us of God's Word at the right moment.
- We are never left without guidance.

This verse assures us that spiritual insight is not self-generated-it is Spirit-led.

Teaching-Reflection:

God confirms His word through peace, scripture, and sometimes others. What He speaks in prayer will often echo through a sermon, a song, or a quiet inner witness. The Holy Spirit is your teacher; His reminders bring clarity, not confusion. Record confirmations as they come; this builds confidence in recognizing His voice.

Key Insight:

Confirmation brings stability. When God repeats a word, He is securing your faith, not questioning your hearing.

Confession to Meditate Upon:

"The Holy Spirit brings clarity to my spirit. I am anchored by peace and guided by truth."

Prayer:

Holy Spirit, thank You for confirming what You've spoken. Thank you for removing every counterfeit voice and strengthening my discernment. Let my confidence rest in You. Amen.

Journal:

List of recent confirmations you've received. How did they deepen your trust in God's guidance?

Day 12 – Spiritual Sensitivity

Proverbs 20:27 (NLT)

"The Lord's light penetrates the human spirit, exposing every hidden motive."

"The spirit of man is the candle of the Lord, searching all the inward parts of the belly." (KJV)

Proverbs 20:27 Summary:

The verse teaches that God uses the human spirit as a lamp to reveal what is hidden within. The "candle" represents illumination; God shines His light through our spirit to expose motives, intentions, wounds, and truth that may be buried deep inside.

Your spirit is not passive; it is a vessel through which God examines, convicts, guides, and reveals. When you become sensitive to the Holy Spirit, He searches your inner being, aligning your heart with His will.

This scripture confirms that discernment begins within. God often speaks inwardly before He confirms outwardly.

Key Truth:

God's light shines through your spirit to reveal truth. Sensitivity to Him brings clarity from the inside out.

Teaching-Reflection:

Sensitivity to the Spirit develops through consistency. The more time you spend in His presence, the quicker you discern His movement. Pay attention to subtle impressions—a sudden thought to pray, a burden for someone, an inner pause before a decision.

Key Insight:

Spiritual sensitivity grows in stillness. What you notice becomes what you nurture.

Confession to Meditate Upon:

"My spirit is alert and responsive to God. I do not ignore divine nudges; I act in faith."

Prayer:

Father, awaken every spiritual sense within me.
Train my heart to notice Your leading and my
body to respond with obedience. In Jesus's name,
amen

Journal:

When was the last time you sensed the Holy Spirit
prompting you? How did you respond?

____

____

____

____

____

____

____

____

____

Day 13 – Discerning the Atmosphere

1 John 4:1 (NIV)

"Dear friends, do not believe every spirit, but test the spirits to see whether they are from God, because many false prophets have gone out into the world."

1 John 4:1 Summary:

This verse teaches that discernment is necessary in the life of every believer. Not every voice, impression, prophecy, or spiritual experience originates from God. Because spiritual influence exists beyond what is seen, believers are instructed to test what they hear and sense.

Testing the spirit means examining whether it aligns with:

- The character of Christ
- The Truth of Scripture
- The fruit it produces (peace, truth, righteousness)

God's Spirit will never contradict His Word or glorify anything above Jesus. Discernment protects you from deception and preserves spiritual maturity.

Teaching-Reflection:

Spiritual discernment separates truth from imitation. Some atmospheres carry divine peace; others carry distraction or deception. You test the spirit by comparing it to Scripture and by observing the fruit it produces. The Spirit of God always exalts Jesus and brings light, not fear.

Key Insight:

Discernment protects destiny. Testing the spirit ensures your agreement aligns with Heaven, not emotion.

Confession to Meditate Upon:

"I walk in discernment and truth. Every atmosphere I enter must submit to the authority of Christ within me."

Prayer:

Lord, sharpen my discernment. Help me identify what is holy and what hinders. Fill every place I stand with Your presence. In Jesus's name, amen

Journal:

Recall a time you sensed unrest or peace entering a space. What did the Holy Spirit reveal about that atmosphere?

Day 14 – The Power of Stillness

Psalm 46:10 (KJV)

"Be still, and know that I am God: I will be exalted among the heathen, I will be exalted in the earth."

Psalm 46:10 Summary:

This verse is both an instruction and an invitation. To "be still" means to cease striving, quiet inner turmoil, and release control. It is a call to rest from anxiety, overthinking, and self-effort.

Stillness positions the heart to recognize God's sovereignty. When you stop wrestling with circumstances and surrender to His authority, clarity replaces confusion. Knowing that He is God produces confidence, peace, and perspective.

Key Truth:

Stillness is not weakness-it is trust. When you quiet yourself before God, you gain deeper awareness of His power and presence.

Teaching-Reflection:

Stillness is not inactivity—it is intentional focus. When you quiet your surroundings, you amplify God's presence. Meditation in His Word transforms anxiety into awareness. The same voice that spoke to Elijah in a whisper desires to meet you in silence.

Key Insight:

Stillness is strength disguised as surrender. In quietness, revelation has room to speak.

Confession to Meditate Upon:

"I find strength in stillness. My spirit hears clearly when my mind rests in God."

Prayer:

Father, teach me the rhythm of rest. Silence the noise around me so I can perceive Your direction. Let Your peace govern my pace. In Jesus's name, amen

Journal:

How can you create more still moments in your daily routine to listen for God's voice?

____

____

____

____

____

____

____

____

____

____

____

____

Day 15 – Meditating on the Word

Joshua 1:8 (NKJV)

"This Book of the Law shall not depart from your mouth, but you shall meditate in it day and night that you may observe to do according to all that is written in it. For then you will make your way prosperous, and then you will have good success"

Joshua 1:8 Summary:

This verse teaches that success in God's Kingdom is rooted in consistent meditation and obedience to His Word. God instructed Joshua to keep the Word on his lips (speaking it), in his mind (meditating on it), and in his actions (doing it).

Prosperity and success here are not worldly ambition, but alignment with God's will. When the Word governs your thoughts and decisions, your path becomes directed and sustained by divine wisdom.

Meditation is not passive reflection—it is intentional focus that produces obedient action.

Key Truth:

When God's Word fills your mouth, mind, and movement, your life aligns with His definition of success.

Teaching-Reflection:

Meditation is the bridge between hearing and obeying. When you ponder God's Word, revelation moves from head to heart. Speaking Scripture aloud imprints it on your spirit. Success follows those who internalize truth until it becomes lifestyle.

Key Insight:

Meditation transforms information into revelation; revelation produces transformation.

Confession to Meditate Upon:

"The Word of God is alive in me. I meditate day and night and walk in divine success."

Prayer:

Lord, engrave Your Word on my heart. Let every thought align with Your promises. Prosper my steps through obedience to truth. In Jesus's name, amen

Journal:

Choose one verse to meditate on this week. What new insight does the Holy Spirit reveal as you repeat and reflect on it?

____

____

____

____

____

____

____

____

Day 16 – Meditation as a Lifestyle

Luke 5:16 (NIV)

"But Jesus often withdrew to lonely places and prayed."

Luke 5:16- Summary:

This verse reveals a powerful spiritual pattern: withdrawal precedes effectiveness. Even though Jesus was surrounded by crowds, miracles, and demands, He intentionally stepped away to spend time in communion with the Father.

His strength, clarity, and authority were sustained by private prayer. Solitude was not escape—it was preparation. In those quiet moments, Jesus aligned His will with the Father's, receiving direction for public ministry.

This scripture teaches that spiritual power flows from private intimacy. What you do in secret fuels what you accomplish in public.

Key Truth:

Consistent withdrawal into God's presence strengthens your public walk. Solitude with the Father sustains success in assignment.

Teaching-Reflection:

Jesus modeled meditation through withdrawal and focus. His strength came not from crowds but from communion. When you cultivate a rhythm of meditating on Scripture and resting in God's presence, your decisions gain clarity and your spirit gains stamina. Meditation is not an event; it is a daily lifestyle that invites revelation.

Key Insight:

Meditation is continual connection—your spirit staying tuned even after prayer ends.

Confession to Meditate Upon:

"I live in continual awareness of God's presence. Meditation is my rhythm of peace and power."

Prayer:

Father, help me build a lifestyle of reflection and stillness. Let every pause become a doorway into Your wisdom. In Jesus's name, amen.

Journal:

What daily moment could you reclaim—morning coffee, commute, walk—to intentionally meditate on God's presence?

____

____

____

____

____

____

____

____

____

____

Day 17 – From Meditation to Manifestation

Proverbs 3:6 (NKJV)

"In all your ways acknowledge Him, And He shall direct your paths."

Proverbs 3:6 Summary:

When you intentionally recognize, honor, and include God in every area of your life, your decisions, plans, relationships, and daily actions, He promises to guide you clearly and lead you in the right direction.

It's an invitation to depend on God completely, not partially. When He is consulted first, confusion decreases and direction becomes clearer.

Meditate on Psalm 37:5; Jeremiah 29:11; Psalm 32:8.

Teaching-Reflection:

Meditation prepares the mind; obedience activates manifestation. When you acknowledge God in each step, revelation turns into results. Divine instruction becomes visible fruit when practiced. Don't rush the process-truth births transformation.

Key Insight:

Revelation without application is information; obedience turns meditation into movement.

Confession to Meditate Upon:

I walk out what I meditate upon. My reflection becomes action, and my obedience produces fruit.

Prayer:

Lord, may what You reveal in secret manifest through my daily walk. Let my life reflect the lessons of Your Word. Amen.

Journal:

Which truth has God repeated lately? How can you act on it today?

Day 18 – The Fragrance of Worship

Ephesians 5:19 (KJV)

"Speaking to yourselves in psalms and hymns and spiritual songs, singing and making melody in your heart to the Lord."

Ephesians 5:19 Summary:

It encourages believers to uplift one another through spiritual songs and to keep a melody of gratitude and praise flowing from the heart to the Lord. Worship is not just corporate; it begins internally and overflows outwardly.

It reminds us that a Spirit-filled life is marked by joy, encouragement, and heartfelt praise.

Teaching-Reflection:

Ministering angels communicates through melody. Songs that rise unbidden in your heart often carry prophetic meaning. When you worship, you align with the rhythm of Heaven, and burdens lift. Worship is warfare that releases peace; lyrics become living words that heal the soul.

Key Insight:

Worship tunes the heart to God's frequency—what you sing, you start to believe.

Confession to Meditate Upon:

"My worship releases revelation. I carry Heaven's song and shift atmospheres with praise."

Prayer:

Lord, fill my heart with Your melody. Let worship silence worry and usher in Your glory. Amen.

Journal:

What lyric or hymn has recently echoed in your spirit? What message might God be speaking through it?

____

____

____

____

____

Day 19 – Prayer That Listens

Jeremiah 33:3 (ESV)

"Call to Me and I will answer you and will tell you great and hidden things that you have not known."

Jeremiah 33:3 Summary:

It's an invitation to seek God in prayer with confidence. When we call on Him, He promises to respond and reveal hidden, powerful truths beyond our current understanding.

It reminds us that revelation comes through relationship, and divine insight is released when we intentionally seek Him.

Teaching-Reflection:

Prayer is conversation, not monologue. After you speak, pause. God often answers in impressions, Scriptures, or sudden peace. Listening prayer trains the heart to value silence as much as speech. What you hear in stillness will sustain you in storms.

Key Insight:

Prayer that's heard transforms requests into relationships.

Confession to Meditate Upon:

"I am quick to hear and slow to speak. God's voice guides my petitions and shapes my perspective."

Prayer:

Holy Spirit, teach me to listen after I pray. Let Your whispers outweigh other voices. In Jesus's name, amen.

Journal:

After your next prayer, wait five minutes in silence. What do you sense or hear?

____

____

____

____

____

Day 20 – Intercession That Changes Atmospheres

Romans 8:26 (NIV)

"In the same way, the Spirit helps us in our weakness. We do not know what we ought to pray for, but the Spirit himself intercedes for us through wordless groans."

Romans 8:26 Summary:

In the same way, the Holy Spirit helps us in our weakness. We do not know what we ought to pray for, but the Holy Spirit prays for us groanings that cannot be expressed in words.

Teaching-Reflection:

There are moments when words fail, yet the Spirit within you prays perfectly. Yielding to that groan births breakthroughs unseen. Intercession is partnership;—Heaven using your vessel to deliver someone else's miracle. Trust the weight of His presence; it's evidence of assignment, not burden.

Key Insight:

When you pray beyond language, you enter the language of power.

Confession to Meditate Upon:

"I am a yielded intercessor. My prayers align with Heaven and release divine outcomes."

Prayer:

Spirit of God, pray through me. Let every groan become glory and every burden birth victory. Amen.

Journal:

Describe a moment when you sensed deep intercession. What fruit or confirmation followed?

____

____

____

____

Day 21 – Keep Listening: A Life Led by His Voice

John 10:27 (KJV)

"My sheep hear My voice, and I know them, and they follow Me."

John 10:27 Summary:

This verse establishes three powerful truths about the believer's relationship with Christ: hearing, intimacy, and obedience.

First, Jesus affirms that His sheep hear His voice-, meaning the ability to recognize God's voice is not reserved for a few; it is the natural privilege of those in relationship with Him.

Second, "I know them" speaks of personal intimacy. Hearing flows from relationships, not ritual. The more you commune with Him, the more familiar His voice becomes.

Third, "they follow Me" reveals that true hearing produces movement. Recognition leads to response.

Key Truth:

Hearing God's voice is a result of a relationship, and following Him is the evidence that you truly heard.

Teaching-Reflection:

Recognizing God's voice is not the end of a journey—it is the beginning of a lifestyle. Each day presents fresh opportunities to listen, obey, and trust. You will not always get it perfectly, but persistence perfects perception. The more you listen, the more familiar His tone becomes.

Key Insight:

A listening life is a leading life. Continual hearing produces continual direction.

Confession to Meditate Upon:

"I walk daily in communion with God. His voice leads, His peace confirms, and His Word sustains me."

Prayer:

Father, thank You for speaking and for teaching me to recognize Your voice. Keep me sensitive, humble, and obedient. May my life forever echo, "Speak, Lord, for Your child hears." Amen.

Journal:

What commitment will you make to continue growing in discernment after these 21 days?

____

____

____

____

____

____

____

____

____

After the 21 Days

Continue Listening

Congratulations on completing **Recognizing When God Speaks: 21-Day Devotional & Confession Guide**. These past days were not just a reading experience—they were an invitation to cultivate a deeper awareness of God's voice.

The goal of this devotional was not only to guide you through 21 days but to help you develop a **lifestyle of spiritual sensitivity**. Recognizing when God speaks becomes clearer as you continue practicing stillness, meditation on His Word, and intentional listening.

Remember, God's voice is not limited to one moment or season. He continues to speak through His Word, through prayer, through dreams, through the inner witness of the Holy Spirit, and through the circumstances that align with His will.

Keep Practicing What You Have Learned

Continue the habits you began during these 21 days:

• Spend daily time in prayer and reflection.
• Meditate on Scripture regularly.
• Write down dreams, thoughts, and impressions
that come during prayer or rest.
• Speak God's truth through confession and
declaration.
• Test every impression by the Word of God.

Over time, you will notice that the voice of God
becomes **more familiar, more comforting, and
more guiding** in your everyday life.

Final Encouragement

Your relationship with God is a journey of
continual discovery. Some days His voice will
come through Scripture, other days through peace
in your spirit, and sometimes through quiet
moments when you simply know He is present.

Remain attentive. Remain teachable. Remain
obedient.

The more you listen, the clearer His voice
becomes.

Final Declaration

"I walk daily in awareness of God's voice. My heart is attentive, my spirit is sensitive, and my life is aligned with His will."

About the Author

Dr. Jacquatta J. Jones, Psy.D.

Dr. Jacquatta J. Jones is an **Ordained Minister of the Gospel and a Licensed Professional Christian Therapist** with a deep passion for helping individuals grow in their relationship with God and discover their identity in Christ. Through years of prayer, counseling, and spiritual insight, she has dedicated her life to guiding others toward healing, clarity, and spiritual transformation.

Dr. Jones is the author of *Recognizing When God Speaks: A Journey into How the Lord Uses Us to Guide, Affirm, and Reveal His Will*. Her work encourages believers to develop spiritual sensitivity and confidence in discerning God's voice through Scripture, prayer, dreams, and the inner witness of the Holy Spirit.

She is also the co-founder of **Restoration Counseling Agency**, where faith-based counseling and guidance are provided to individuals, couples, and families seeking restoration and spiritual growth.

Through her writing, teaching, and counseling ministry, Dr. Jones continues to inspire people to pursue a deeper walk with God and to live a life led by His voice.

Stay Connected

Dr. Jacquatta J. Jones founded Power of

Meditation in God's Presence, a gathering designed to invite God's people into a deeper awareness of His voice through intentional meditation on His Word. These times of reflection, prayer, and spiritual stillness help believers grow in discernment and strengthen their relationship with the Lord.

Additional gatherings and opportunities to participate will be announced.

For questions, updates or follow-up information, please contact:

Email: Jacquattajj@gmail.com
Additional event details: To Be Announced (TBA)

Encouragement from the Author

My prayer is that this devotional has strengthened your confidence in recognizing when God speaks. May your heart remain open, your spirit attentive, and your life continually aligned with His voice.

www.ingramcontent.com/pod-product-compliance
Lightning Source LLC
Chambersburg PA
CBHW051944150726
47999CB00006B/2363